KU-300-789

PLAYS

Mobile phoney

Barbara Mitchelhill

Published in association with
The Basic Skills Agency

Hodder & Stoughton

A MEMBER OF THE HODDER HEADLINE GROUP

Acknowledgements
Cover: Photodisc
Illustrations: Mike Bell

Orders: please contact Bookpoint Ltd, 130 Milton Park, Abingdon, Oxon OX14
4SB. Telephone: (44) 01235 827720, Fax: (44) 01235 400454. Lines are open from
9.00–6.00, Monday to Saturday, with a 24 hour message answering service. Email
address: orders@bookpoint.co.uk

British Library Cataloguing in Publication Data
A catalogue record for this title is available from The British Library

ISBN 0 340 86941 0

First published 1999
This edition published 2002
Impression number   10 9 8 7 6 5 4 3 2 1
Year   2007 2006 2005 2004 2003 2002

Typeset by Fakenham Photosetting Ltd, Fakenham, Norfolk.
Printed in Great Britain for Hodder & Stoughton Educational, a division of
Hodder Headline Plc, 338 Euston Road, London NW1 3BH by Athenaeum Press,
Gateshead, Tyne & Wear.

About the play

The People
- Kev
- Jade

The Place
*The High Street of the town where **Kev** and **Jade** live.*

The Scene
*__Kev__ is talking to his friend, **Rich**, near to a phone box.*
*Down the street, **Jade** is standing at a bus stop.*

Kev   Don't stand there looking at me, Rich!
Get into the phone box.
And remember what I said.
When you see me talking to Jade,
ring the number I gave you.
OK?
This should do it.
I reckon she'll be dead impressed.

He walks down the street.

Hi, Jade.
Fancy meeting you!
Are you on your way home from work?

Jade   Hi, Kev.
Yeah. I've been working late.
What are you doing?

Kev   I'm on my way home from a meeting.

It's been a really hard day.

You know how it is.

Still, it's good for business.

My briefcase is bulging with orders.

Jade   Are you in sales now?

I thought you worked at the

chicken factory.

Kev   Me? Oh that was ages ago.

No.

I've got my own business now.

Jade   What kind?

Kev   Oh … wheeling and dealing.

I don't care

just as long as I can earn

loads of money,

have a nice car,

holidays abroad.

You know.

Jade   Where is your car?

Kev   It's er ...
it's in the garage for a wax and clean.
I don't have time to do it myself.
I'm too busy.
And you've got to have an
impressive car
when you're in business.

Jade   You're quite a surprise,
aren't you, Kev?

Kev   Yeah.
The business is booming.

Jade   I thought your brother
was the businessman
in your family.
Lewis is dead successful, isn't he?
I always liked him.

Kev's mobile phone rings.

Kev   Sorry about this Jade.
It's probably business.
Hello?

Oh hello, Monica.

It's my secretary.
I won't be a minute.

What did James think of that price I
quoted?

Pause

25 grand wasn't out of his range, was it?

Pause

I didn't think it would be!

Pause

Right.
Will you send him a contract
straight away?
I'll sign it when I get back to the office.

Bye.

*Switches off the phone and puts it
in his pocket.*

Right then, Jade.
What were we talking about?

Jade Your business.
You seem to be doing all right,
I'm impressed.

Kev Just wait.
You ain't seen nothin' yet, Babe!
I'll be a millionaire before I'm 25.

Jade Oh yeah?
It must be quite a business you've got.

Kev It is.
Come and have a drink with me
and I'll tell you all about it.

Jade I don't think so, Kev.
Thanks all the same.
I don't like pubs.

Kev I didn't mean a pub.

I don't like pubs myself.
No – we could go to the Waveley Hotel.
It's just round the corner.

Jade   Well …

Kev   Go on.

Jade   Well, I could have a cocktail.
That's what everybody drinks in
London,
isn't it?
I read it in a magazine.

Kev   Then I'll buy you a cocktail at the
Waveley.

Jade   Oh all right then.
Go on.

They walk down the road
to a large expensive hotel
where Kev orders two drinks from the bar.

8

Kev There you are, Jade.

One special cocktail.

There's enough fruit in that

to open a greengrocer's shop.

Jade Thanks.

Aren't you having one?

Kev No. I'll stick to lager.

Jade Cheers.

She takes a mouthful.

Kev I'm really glad you came, Jade.

I've been wanting to ask you out for

ages.

Jade Really?

She takes another mouthful

Oooh!

That's delicious.

I've never tasted anything like it.

Like lemonade with cherries in it.

She takes another mouthful.

Kev   You're a real looker, you are, Jade.
I suppose 'like' attracts 'like'
– know what I mean?
Beautiful babe.
Successful businessman.

Jade   Your Lewis is a real looker.
But he's never asked me out, you know.
I wish he would.
Do you think he fancies me?
(*giggling*)
Oooh!
I could get used to these cocktails.
But you don't get much in a glass do
you?
Hardly a mouthful.

She drains the glass.

I'd love another one.

Kev	Well … er …
Jade	Please!
	Unless it's too expensive, Kev.
	I can always pay for my own drink if …
Kev	(*laughing*)
	No. No.
	I'm loaded, Jade.
	I've probably got more money than Lewis.
	Money doesn't mean anything to me.
Jade	In that case, let's have a meal in the restaurant.
	I've heard it's brilliant.
	We could celebrate your business deal.
	That would be nice, wouldn't it?
Kev	Don't you have to go home?
	Won't your mum have tea ready?
Jade	Oh no.
	I've got my own flat now.
	I'd much rather eat here than cook for myself.

It's gorgeous, isn't it?
All those waiters with their bow ties.
Gorgeous!

Kev Oh … Right …
I'll go and see if they've got a table.

He walks away
but nips into the loo
where he takes out the mobile phone.

Rich, is that you?

Pause

Thank goodness you're home.

Pause

Yeah! I pulled …

Pause

Yeah, I know it's great
but I've got a problem.

Pause

I'm in the Waveley Hotel.

Pause

That's right.
That really posh place.
I had to bring her here.
She wouldn't go to the pub.

Pause

I know it's expensive.
I've just bought a cocktail
and it cost me a week's wages.
That's why I'm ringing you, Rich.
She wants to have a meal here
and I'm skint.

What can I do?

Pause

Isn't Greg having a party tonight?
That might just save my bacon.
And it's free.
The only snag is – he didn't invite me.

Pause

I suppose I *could* gatecrash.
His party's are dead impressive.
Loads of booze and good food.
A party's loads better
than a meal at the Waveley Hotel,
isn't it?
And cheaper!

Pause

Right.

I know what you can do, Rich.
Ring me on the mobile in two minutes.
I'll get it sorted.
Thanks mate.
I owe you.

He returns to Jade.

Sorry I've been so long.
They're heavily booked in the
restaurant.

Jade Don't tell me you didn't get a table.
Kev 'Course I did.
I just had to slip
the head waiter a few quid.
But we'll have to wait for a bit.
Jade Oh well.
I'll have another of those cocktails then.
Kev Hang on a couple of minutes
and I'll go to the bar.
I haven't finished my lager yet.
Jade But your glass is nearly empty.

Kev   No, it's not.
          There's still some in there.
Jade   Well if there is, I can't see it.

Mobile rings.

Kev   Hello.

          It's my secretary again.
          Excuse me.
          I won't be a minute.

          Hi Monica.

          Pause

          Greg Fitzsimmons?
          Oh no!
          I'd forgotten his party.
          Thanks for reminding me.
          I've just booked a table at the Waveley.
          Never mind.

Greg's too important a client to turn down.
I'm sure Jade won't mind going with me.

Pause

Yes, I'll make sure
I sign all those contracts tomorrow.
'Bye Monica.

Puts the phone away.

Jade   Do you know Greg Fitzsimmons?
         I bet you know everybody!
Kev   I used to go to school with him … er …
         and he's an important business client.
Jade   He's dead cool, he is.
         Almost as cool as your brother.
Kev   Some might say that, I suppose.
         Anyway, it's his party tonight.
         I'd forgotten about it.
         He's been asking me for ages.

| | I've got to go
| | but you can come too if you want to.
| **Jade** | Oh you do live an exciting life, Kev!
| | I love parties.

They leave the hotel and go to Greg's flat.

| **Jade** | Pity we had to get here by bus.
| | Still, it sounds like a great party.
| | You could hear that stereo down the road.
| | Is this Greg's flat?
| **Kev** | Yeah. That's it.
| | I've been here loads of times.
| **Jade** | There's a note pinned to the door.
| **Kev** | Oh yeah.
| **Jade** | Look, Kev – it says
| | **Everybody who was invited**
| | **is now inside my flat.**
| | What's he mean?
| | We're not inside, are we?
| **Kev** | Huh!

It's just one of Greg's jokes.

You know what he's like.

Jade It's not a joke.

Look what it says underneath.

Gatecrashers get lost!

Kev Well, I don't think it means me.

Jade I think it does, Kev.

Look what it says at the bottom.

This means you too Kevin Shipley!

Mobile rings unexpectedly.

Kev Hello?

Pause

It's my secretary again.

What a busy night!

I won't be a minute, Jade.

Jade snatches the phone from Kev.

Jade   Let me speak to her.

Hello? It's Jade here.
Who's that?

Pause

Lewis!
Kev said it was his secretary.
I didn't believe him somehow.

Pause

No.
I didn't think he had one.

Pause

What a cheek!

Pause

What a wimp.

Pause

No.
I'm going home right now.
I'm fed up.

Pause

Right ... Oh yes.
That sounds good to me.
See ya then.

Switches mobile off.

Kev   I can explain, Jade.
Jade   No. I'll explain.
Everything you told me is a lie.
The business.
Your money.
Everything.

Even your mobile phone isn't your
own.
You stole it from your brother
this morning.

Kev   So you don't fancy me then?

Jade   No, Kev, I don't fancy you one little bit.
What's more,
Lewis is coming round to pick me up
in ten minutes.

Kev   Right then.
Give him his mobile, will you?
… and tell him it didn't work!